Work Life Balance

iland business publishing specialises in the area of reference guides for readers seeking practical information to improve themselves in careers, finance, and other related core business topics. We bring our readers the information they need to stay in step with required skills and techniques.

Our authors are experts in their fields and deliver well-written, easy-to-follow, yet comprehensive books that inform, advise, and educate.

Work Life Balance

iland business pages

Work Life Balance is published by iland business pages

Copyright © 2013 by iland business pages

All rights reserved. No part of this book shall be reproduced, stored in a retrieval system, or transmitted by any means, electronic, mechanical, photocopying, recording, or otherwise, without written permission from the publisher. No patent liability is assumed with respect to the use of the information contained herein. Although every precaution has been taken in preparation of this book, the publisher and author assume no responsibility for errors or omissions. Nor is any liability assumed for damages resulting from the use of the information contained herein.

All terms mentioned in this book that are known to be trademarks or service marks have been appropriately capitalized. Iland business pages cannot attest to the accuracy of this information. Use of a term in this book should not be regarded as affecting the validity of any trademark or service mark.

Every effort has been made to make this book as complete and as accurate as possible, but no warranty or fitness is implied. The information provides is on an „as is" basis. The author and the publisher shall have neither liability nor responsibility to any person or entity with respect to any loss or damages arising from the information contained in this book.

ISBN-13: 978-1482608830

ISBN-10: 1482608839

1h pro 009

Table of Contents

Work Life Balance

Why should you read this Book?	09
Work – Life Balance – The Diagnosis	11
How does the Imbalance affect your life?	15
Physical Effects of Stress	16
Emotional Effects of Stress	19
Stress Effects on Relationships	21
Are you dedicated or addicted to your Work?	25
Which side rules, Work Or Home?	26
Reclaim your Space and Time – Learn To Set Limits	35
10 Myths That Work Against You	41
10 Tips to improve your Productivity	57
Waking Up Exercises	71
You need to get back in Control	75
Meditation as a Tool against Stress	77
Six Baby Steps to optimize your Efficiency	91
20 Work Life Balances Ideas	99
Conclusion	115

Why should you read this book?
Work Life Balance

The world today has changed a lot from the world that we knew some 5-6 decades ago. At that time, when a couple decided to live in or marry, the man would most likely to be the provider of the family and the woman would be the homemaker. Both had more or less clear-cut roles and expectations. Jobs were as demanding, with many men doing overtime to ensure a better income for the family. However, since the women stayed at home, the children rarely lacked care or attention. Work – family life balance was a problem at that time as well; but it was managed with vacations, traditional get-togethers, and other family intensive activities where the whole family spent quality time together.

In modern days, where consumerism has reached gargantuan proportions money has become one of the most important 'to-have' commodities. Recession, college dropouts, ready availability of cheap human resources has made jobs difficult to find. Whatever jobs are available - unless you are highly qualified and have adequate experience and expertise – come with low paychecks, which means you would need to work more than one job, or longer hours.

Add to all this, commuting time and overtime and you will end up with absolutely no time to even rest; forget about time to spend with your family. This is not the worst part; there is more. Today both life partners work equally hard and the children are generally taken care of nannies and babysitters. Both parents try to make up for the lack of quality time with gifts, higher allowance, and more permissiveness. However, the guilt and overall personal dissatisfaction that they are neglecting the family remains. Sooner or later, this dissatisfaction spills over into the professional life and affects it negatively.

To regain your mental peace, you will need to pay more attention to your relationships, to your spouse, children, bonding time with your family and so on. In other words, unless there you find a way to balance your work and home-life you will end up feeling miserable, dissatisfied and frustrated in every aspect of your life.

This book attempts to show you how you can achieve this work-life balance. This book is designed to stop you from reaching that point of no return where you lose your peace of mind, your family, job satisfaction and even your job. This book is designed to save your life – literally.

Work Life Balance – A Diagnosis

Before we go any further we need to check out where are you with this issue. Is your work and personal life balanced well enough, or is it already a lopsided affair? Let us start with a questionnaire that will help diagnose the problem correctly. Answer with 'Yes' and 'No'.

a) Does your work take more time of your day than you would want to give?

b) Do you carry your work home and continue to encroach on to your family time (say, do you have to finish projects, follow up on business phone calls, emails, and so on)?

If you answer yes, how many hours per week are used in this manner?
- 1-4 hours
- 5-9 hours
- 10+ hours

If you are a home-entrepreneur how many hours over the acceptable 40 hours per week you put in?
- 1-4 hours
- 5-9 hours
- 10+ hours

c) Do you often find yourself worrying about work when you are supposed to spend time with your spouse/ family (dinner time/ watching TV together/ vacations/ etc.?

d) Have you sacrificed things you used to love to do because you do not have any more time due to work?

If yes, how many of these pleasure activities you have forgone?
    1-3 activities
    4-6 activities
    7+ activities

e) Do you have the time to exercise, eat healthy and sleep well at night?

f) Are you satisfied with how much time you are giving your loved ones?

g) Do you find the time to do personal things that are important to you (or do you postpone them indefinitely because you are too busy with work)?

h) Would you say that you are happy – in general terms?

i) Would you say that this is the life you would dreamt for yourself (are you content with how things are?

j) If you could, would you want to live in this way forever?

The score:

Give yourself 1 point for every 'Yes' answered to questions 1-5; the lower the score the better.

Give yourself 1 point for every 'No' answered to questions 6-10; the lower the score the better.

If you score higher than 3, it means trouble; it means that your work is stealing your life away from you and unless you plan to do something about it right now, things will go worse.

How Does The Imbalance Affect Your Life

In you are going through life focusing solely on your work and neglecting your family life, you will sooner or later feel restless, frustrated, anxious, unhappy and dysfunctional. While it is true, that some people find fulfillment in the success they achieve in the professional life, if they do not have enough happiness drawn from their relationships to balance the professional high, sooner than later they would feel acute frustration. This frustration would gradually but surely spill in their professional life and affect that too. In the end, the person who starts out as a workaholic would end lonely, frustrated and quite unfulfilled no matter how successful professionally.

Too much work would cause stress to build up to dangerous levels; and stress is a definite killer. Normally stress would and could be neutralized by pleasurable activities such as time spent with spouse, children, hobbies, vacations, meditation, and so on.

Physical Effects Of Stress

Stress is a very serious issue and if not countered in time, it could affect your health seriously, sometimes with fatal results. This is why today, the most important and golden keywords you keep hearing are de-stressing, meditation, balance of work and personal life.

If and when you are stressed you will experience one or more of the following symptoms:

- **Eating Disorders** – you would either start eating too much or you would start hating the sight of food. The result is that you would either put on weight or lose weight drastically. Of course, along with this disorder would come many associated health problems.

- **Fatigue** – you would find that you feel fatigued no matter what you do. Even when you have not done much physically, you would still feel drained out and lacking the energy required to get through the day. No matter what you do, you would feel pooped.

- **High Blood Pressure** – today, more and more young people (in the age bracket of 30-45 years old) suffer from high blood pressure. While some would point out that this would be the result of unhealthy eating habits of today's population, doctors admit that stress is quoted as the primary factor for this problem.

- **Heart Problems** – just 3-4 decades ago, heart problems, cardiac arrests, strokes, angina and so on were problems experienced by people who passed their 55th year. Today, the age has come down to as low as 35. Why? Because stress is causing artery clogging and cholesterol build up, which in turn leads to severe heart problems; sometime fatal.

- **Infections, Allergies and Skin Problems** – stress lowers your immune system and makes you vulnerable to infections, allergies and **skin** problems. You will find that many people suffer from asthmatic attacks, flues, fungal and bacterial infection, various allergies, skin rashes (such as eczema, psoriasis, etc.), and so on. With the immune system dysfunctional the body is vulnerable to all types of germs and viral attacks.

- **Diarrhea/ Constipation** - **stress** heavily interferes with digestion and absorption of food matter. As a result you would end up either suffering from constipation or loose motions (diarrhea) intermittently without any apparent causes.

- **Sleep Disorders** – stress keeps the body in the flight-or-fight survival mode and hence, you would feel high strung all the time. This mode of existence would not allow you to relax enough so you could sleep well. Most people who are affected by stress cannot sleep the required 4-6 hours per night. For others, sleep becomes the safety cocoon and find that they feel sleepy/dozy all the time; however, even if they sleep more than 10 hours, they would still feel awful.

- **Fertility And Sexual Disorders** – stress holds your body in the fight-or-flight mode, which requires that the blood supply be primarily directed to the most vital organs. Skin, reproduction system are among the non-vital organs/ systems that get second hand attention at such time. If stress levels are maintained at high levels, fertility levels, sexual health, libido start suffering.

- **Aging Signs** - the skin, hair and nails are other aspects that would suffer greatly during this time. The hair would look dull, the nails would be brittle, skin overall will show signs of aging. Add to this the fact that most people in today's age smoke, drink alcohol and eat unhealthy and you could draw your own inference of the impact these issues added to stress can do to the skin.

- **Inflammation** - stress lowers the immune systems owing to which inflammation takes over the body. It starts with simple headaches (inflammation of sinus membranes) and gradually spreads to back pain, joint pain and generally feeling pain all over the body.

Emotional Effects Of Stress

Besides the physical effects caused by stress – which are most often faster and easier to observe – there are emotional effects, too. Here are a few that would develop gradually owing to overload of stress:

- **Depression And Mood Swings** – continuous stress would keep you mentally tense through the day. The stress would influence the hormone production in the body, which couples with sleep and eating disorders would result in sudden mood swings and depression.

- **Anxiety Attacks And Nervousness** – no matter how good you are at **your** work, continuous stress would result in unexplained feelings of 'butterflies in the stomach', which if left untreated will culminate into anxiety attacks.

- **Memory And Concentration Problems** – you will observe that stress would **affect** your memory seriously. You would suddenly forget things that you would have ordinarily remembered effortlessly. You would also not be able to focus or concentrate for too long on any matter.

- **Increase Of Substance Abuse** – stress and the uncomfortable feelings it causes would push you to search for ways to find cures. **Unfortunately**, most people do not look at meditation, hobbies, cutting down on work, and healthy food. They take the help of cigarettes, coffee, alcohol, and other substance abuse, which add to the trouble creating an unbreakable vicious circle.

Stress Effects On Relationships

Look at the symptoms described above. You can imagine that any person who is going through such a lot would not be great company in any circumstances. As a result, relationships start suffering. The first relationships to be sacrificed would be with family, because they are whom we all take most for granted. Then, relationships with friends would suffer and in the end – if no measures are taken – professional relationships would suffer as well. Some of the symptoms you would notice with your relationships are:

- **Repeated Arguments** – say, you are already tense with your nerves stretched on end and something happens at home. You suddenly explode into an argument causing your children and/ or spouse draw away from you. With time, you will find that your family moves away so far that you can no longer bridge the gap.

- **Road Rage** – you find there is a lot of suppressed anger in you. You may suppress it successfully at workplaces and home for a while. Finding no outlet, the frustration builds up and suddenly manifests itself on the road towards fellow drivers and/ or passengers. You take your anger out on them, which makes you feel good initially – but not for long.

- **Social Activities Suffer** – you do not have the time or the mood to socialize and hence, you are having trouble keeping contact with relatives and friends. You become a recluse socially, rarely meeting people and gradually moving away from all social contacts.

- **Conflict At Work Place** – left unattended, the suppressed anger continues to build up until you would be like a dynamite stick with a lighted fuse. Anything around you could trigger an explosion. You start having conflicts with your fellow worker, and sometime even with the boss.

- **Violence Raises Its Ugly Head** – stress takes over the mind and keeps your nerves stretched to no end. Any argument now can and often will trigger violence. Whether at home or at the workplace you will be known as a person with a short fuse whose company needs to be avoided at all cost.

- **Divorce/ Erosion Or End Of Close Relationships** – your spouse wants a divorce; your live-in partner feels he/ she cannot continue with you. Friends shun you as you become feeling sour that you no longer make a good company. You find yourself at the end of it alone; no love, no friends, no children, no colleagues – nothing.

- **Frequent Job Changes** – stress would not make you a model worker even if you work night and day. Your inability to work with your co-workers without entering into an argument, the fact that you would always be stressed would get you into trouble all the time at your workplace. This would make it difficult for you to keep your job for long, even if you work harder.

Are You Dedicated Or Addicted To Your Work?

Why are you allowing your work to take over your whole life and wreck it? Are you dedicated to your profession or the type of work you are doing? Or is this rather an addiction that you cannot get away from? It is important to know and understand the difference between being dedicated to your work – and hence, neglecting your family for it – and being addicted to your work and sacrificing your family for it.

Which Side Rules, Work Or Home?
-
A Small Quiz

This is a wonderfully effective quiz that will give you an idea or spell it out for you the way it is. Surprisingly, in the majority of cases the affected person does not really know that there is a problem of such major magnitude until the worst of the symptoms manifest such as a divorce, job loss, kids becoming wild and so on. Take the quiz and find out what is your story. Answer with a number on a 1-5 scale where 5 means 'Always' and 1 means 'Never' – with the gradients in between accordingly.

Always				**Never**
5	**4**	**3**	**2**	**1**

At Home,

- do you hear your family complaining often that they are not getting enough of you?
- do these complaints/ demands on your time by your family make you anxious/ irritated/ angry?
- do you resentment when you have to do household chores or spend time with the family?

- do you feel that your family should be more adapting, more tolerant, more adjusting to the needs of your work/ career?

Subtotal Part One: _____

At Work,

- do you irked by the fast that your income is not sufficient for your needs?
- do you feel guilty that you are putting in so much time and effort in building your career?
- do you find it frustrating that you have to take your work home at the end of the day because there is always so much more to do?
- do you find yourself worrying that your work robs you from the happiness you would have otherwise with your family?

Subtotal Part Two: _____

On Personal Front,

- do you feel that you never get any time free for yourself?
- do you feel guilty when you take a break or vacation?
- do you wish that you had the time for more exercise?
- do you feel that you are not able to get enough time to ever do what you really want to do?

Subtotal Part Three: _____

What Does The Score Say:

A total score of **less than 20** indicates that you found just the right way to balance family, career and personal needs. A high score in only one area indicates you need to re-organize your life so that area takes less of your time and energy.

21-30 indicates a good balance with some need for improvement

31-40 indicates a fair balance

41-50 shows that **you** are barely managing the juggling act of home, career and personal needs.

Make the effort to identify what area needs your attention and work hard to get there. Unless you get the balance in your life, nothing will save you in the end from being lonely, disillusioned and unfulfilled.

It is very important'that you understand what drives you towards putting in too much time at work. The difference between 'being addicted' and 'being dedicated' is just that the former will make you feel guiltier than the latter. However, both are bad and unless you find a way to balance work and your home life. Sometimes, even quality of time counts.

Say, you are very busy and have a very demanding job or profession. If you manage to extricate yourself long enough to spend some super-quality time with your family, it would definitely compensate for the busy times. When you say, 'quality time' it is time that is 100% for your family. If you want to really counter the busy time with quality time, you have to give your 100% to your family for that allotted time span.

This means no work, to talk about work, no worrying about work, NOTHING that connects you to work. This means that you do whatever you do with all your heart and enjoy it. You cannot fake enjoyment; you need to find that thing you can do with your family – and sometimes with yourself – that you totally enjoy.

Are You Addicted To Your Job?

Okay. What if? Is it bad? Well, by definition, all "addictions" are indeed bad. Addictions are something that takes over your mind and gradually make you lose control of yourself and your environment. Once the addiction takes over, you can no longer do what you want, see what is good for you, or change anything. You are just helpless in the clutches of the addiction and unless you recognize, accept that it controls you, and try to fight it out, you will lose everything you hold dear in your life.

What Caused The Addiction?

It is important that you realize what caused the addiction. Any addiction starts with a feel-good factor. You will like something – in the beginning – so much that you would want to do it again and again to enjoy that feeling of happiness. It is very important that you find what caused the addiction in the first place. What made you feel so good that you needed to do it more and more, again and again. Once you identify what made you happy, you need to find other ways to get to that point of happiness.

(1) The Personal Satisfaction

It could be the personal satisfaction that you feel when you get your job well done. It could be the satisfaction you enjoy when you are appreciated for your proficiency in your work. It could be the satisfaction that you get from doing your job better than anyone else.

(2) The Money

It could be the money that you are making on your job. Sometimes, money can be very addictive. If you are making a good amount, it sometimes acts like a motivator to make more. You start liking earning the money so much that you never want to stop.

(3) The Recognition

Another factor that could be extremely addictive is the recognition you get from your work Sometimes, this is more addictive than any other factor. With this the more you get, the more you crave for it and the high one gets from recognition is often insatiable.

(4) *The Identity*

Sometimes, at least in the initial stages the professions or job gives you your identity. This can become gradually everything you are and when it does, it takes over and total precedence over every aspect of your life. This one among most dangerous addictions, for even considering leaving this would mean that you go against your very identity and hence, most difficult to get rid of.

(5) *The Projected Family*

For some, the workplace becomes the projected family that they would always want. In such a case, they would feel they'd betray their trust if they did not give them 100% of their time and hence, it'd be like they are cheating. This addiction too, requires a lot of effort and work to get rid of.

Are You Dedicated To Your Job?

To be dedicated to your job is not that bad a problem. In fact, this is more a positive aspect that negative. If it is dedication that drives you to work more and more, then all you need to do is transfer a little of that dedication to your present family.

This normally happens because the job comes much earlier in life than your family and for most people it becomes the first family, the first priority. It becomes a matter of habit that you pay more attention to your job and just offer the other part of your life whatever time and energy remains.

Sometimes, the job does require long hours of work. Professionals such as doctors, lawyers, scientists, researchers, etc. are indeed demanding and exhausting. Here, most people feel trapped since they know they cannot reduce the intensity of their work or the hours they need to put in. Yet, they also know that they have to pay attention to their families as well.

This clash of priorities normally builds up stress since it feeds on guilt and on both accounts. The person feels guilty when at home because they feel they are neglecting their job; when at a job, they feel guilty about their home since they know they are not giving quality time to their families. In this case, dedication becomes costly and a permanent fuel for stress. Hence, unless you find a way to balance your work and home life, you will never be able to get rid of the stress.

It is worthwhile to keep in mind that stress that does not reduce by itself, neither it will ever remain constant. It will grow and grow as it feeds upon itself and as with compound interests, it continues to build until it totally overwhelms you. This is why you need to fight stress with all your might. In many ways when you fight stress, you actually find the key to balance your work life and home life for you gain new perspective on what is important and what is not and how to handle both aspects.

Reclaim Your Space And Time

—

Learn To Set Limits

Sometimes it is hard to learn to pay enough attention to ourselves while we focus on the needs of others around us; this could be family, work, friends. If you make it a habit to view other people's needs as more important than your own, it can be extremely hard to regain control and set limits where necessary. The following workout sheets will help you recognize some of these critical areas where you might be cheating yourself.

Workout No1:

Make a list of all the things that - in your opinion – must be done in your life. This is not compartmentalized; include the needs / demands from all areas that affect your life, i.e. work, colleagues, spouse, children, relatives, religious denomination, and so on.

Work Out No2:

Make a second list, but on this list you write down ONLY your own needs. The list should look something like this:

I need

- more free time to indulge in XYZ hobby;
- more freedom to do my work the way I want it;

- someone I could trust with my feelings;
- more help to raise my children;
- more time with my wife/ husband/ kids;
- more help with my work;
- more help with my household needs; and so on.

Draw two large, same size circles (or you could use your computer for this purpose) and name them Circle No1 and Circle No2. Now divide Circle1 in so many pieces as you described in a Work Out No 1. It should look like a pie-chart. Take Circle No2 and now divide it according to what you want your life to be.

Look at both the circles now, and decide what measures you need to take to ensure that you could reach to the point where you could lead the life you envisaged for yourself. Now, make a **third list** with all the things that you need to do to ensure that you would reach to that place where you could lead the life you want for yourself.

Once you have set limits in areas that you feel are dragging you down, try to stick to it. It will not be easy – so do not think that these exercises would have you change your life overnight. It will be an uphill task, and you should be prepared to struggle for a while until you reach that perfect-balance point in your life.

Important: Set SMART Goals

You need to set some SMART goals and then take it one step at a time. SMART is an acronym for **S**pecific – **M**easurable – **A**ctionable – **R**elevant & Relevant – **T**imebound. This means that your goals should:

- Have SPECIFIC outcome stated; you should know what you have planned to achieve and then break it into small goals. For example, you will start out with a statement like **"I want to start painting."** When this goal would have been achieved, you would have started painting.

- The goal you set should be measurable. In this case, let us start with ONE painting. Hence, the goal until now should look like this, **"I want to start painting as a hobby. I need to start with at least one painting done."**

- Plan the actionable steps. In order to move from the point where you are not painting to the point where you are painting, what do you need? You will need all such items that are normally used by one who paints. You will also need to take out time that would be allocated for painting. Now, your goal would like this – "**I want to start painting as a hobby. I need to start with at least one painting done on this Sunday.**"

- The goal should have a time schedule allotted to it. In the end, the goal should look like this, "**I**

want to start painting as a hobby. I need to start with at least one painting done on this Sunday. I plan to have this painting completed within 4-6 Sundays."

So, here you are. You have a plan to move from point A – where you are not painting as a hobby – to point B, where you are now painting regularly as a hobby. Within maximum 6 weeks from the day you started out to act on this goal, you will have ONE painting completed.

Use this model and roll out. Have a time frame within which you have moved from Point A to Point B, where point A is where you are right now and point B is where you want to be. You want change? You need to take action; you need to take that action right now. The secret of successful people is simple – they act NOW. You want to achieve, start right NOW to move into that direction.

Have a picture in your mind of what it should be and then fill it up with tiny actionable steps. Now walk the path and get there. That is all there is to it.

Setting a goal and acting on it is not all that difficult. You will find it extremely rewarding when you would have achieved the goal you have set out to achieve within the time limit set. The trick is to start small and move on to bigger things gradually until you have a complete change in your lifestyle. Your 'Point A' in this case is the life you are leading where work overwhelms the family time. Your 'Point B' is where you would want to be, i.e. the person who has achieved the perfect balance between work and family life.

So, to revise and ensure that you have internalized this process, let us revise what was learnt here:

Set up clear and specific goals. Envision how you want it to become.

Set up indicators that you could measure at the end of each step you take. It is important that you enjoy the feeling that you have achieved something every time you complete a mini-step in your goal.

Take action. Start NOW.

Walk the path with baby steps; it is important that you do not feel stressed by the change; rather you feel good and motivated with every step that you take in the direction you want.

Set a time limit. You cannot measure your achievement unless there is a time limit. Hence, your goals should have a set and non-negotiable time limit, so you know how much time you have to get there.

By the time you reach the set time limit, you would have achieved the goal.

10 Myths That Work Against You – Beware

You are the only one in this world who feels that he is paying too much attention to his work and too less to its family. There are, in fact, millions of people out there who suffer greatly because of this particular problem They want to change, but cannot and/ or will not because they believe in a few myths that holds them back.

You need to know about these myths so you would not hold back from seeking avenue and methods to balance you're the time you spend at work and that you would like to spend on your life (family).

Myth 1: Success Means Mastering Multitasking

There is a strong believe today among people in all professions and level of work that you cannot be called successful unless you master the art of multitasking.

Nothing can be further from the truth. You would think that multitasking means doing two or more tasks at the same time. However, this is not so. What you are actually doing is switch quickly between any two or more tasks that you are trying to complete simultaneously. The human brain is meant to focus on one thing at a time, hence what actually happens when you multitask, is shifting your attention rapidly from one task to another.

Normally this would that you are saving time and achieving much more in the give time. But this is not true. Since you are switching your attention, you actually shut off the attention you pay to one task and set it to another. Every time you do this, there is a slight time gap where your brain reloads the information about task 1/ task2/ task 3 and so on. Hence, every time you switch between the tasks you chose to multitask, you are losing time.

Hence, if you would do one task at a time, one AFTER the other and NOT one ALONG with the other, you would need much less time; you would complete that task and have a lot more time left on your hand, plus you will feel relaxed and comfortable and not fatigued and overcome as one feels after a busy day of multi-tasking.

So, you want to work more and better avoid as much as possible multi-tasking. Try organizing your calendar to do one thing at a time. Give that one task that you take up your full attention and complete it before moving on to another. Do not check your emails or attend the phone while you are working. For email have 3-4 schedules per day to read and answer them; for telephone, have an answering machine connected so you could screen your calls and answer only those that just have to be answered.

Make these few almost insignificant changes, and you will be amazed with how much work you are able to get done after this.

Myth 2: Pressure Helps You Work Better, Faster

This one is a killer, because it is partially true. Pressure, and imminent deadlines do make you work better. The heightened adrenaline does release the innermost reserves in you and unleashes your inner potential. It is true that in a heightened excited state you do more and do better. However, this state is definitely NOT one you would like to be every day, day after day, month after month. This is a state of stress; and the heightened senses are the result of the activation of the fight or fight syndrome.

The pressure and/ or imminent deadlines are interpreted by your mind as life-threatening situations – which often are, for if you miss on a deadline you might actually lose your job – and with it, comes plenty of trouble. When your mind and body perceives a survival threat, it declares a state of emergency where blood is pulled away (only minimum is left flowing) from all the non-vital organs and pumped into the vital organs such as brain, heart, lungs, kidneys and liver.

The danger in the background pushes your mind and body into a heightened state of energy; as massive shots of adrenaline start being produced and released into to blood. You feel like you can jump over a building if you have to – at such times. Accordingly you work like 5 people put together and the job you do is WOW!

Hence, it is good to be challenged by deadlines SOMETIMES since it does bring the best in you. The keyword here is 'sometimes'. If you are in that state 24x7, you are courting heavy trouble for your body cannot stay healthy for long in the fight-or-flight mode. Physiologically, when the blood is pulled away from the non-vital organs such as stomach, organs of the reproductive system, spleen, gall bladder, pancreas, eyes, skin and the like – if this is sustained over long periods, these organs will start malfunctioning.

Hence, you will develop problems with digestion, sexual function, eyesight, and so on. This explains why stressed people have so many issues with food, digestion, acidity and so on. They also are more often than not suffering from sexual dysfunction – decreased libido, infertility, erectile dysfunction and so on. In the long run, this heightened state of function would cost you very dearly.

With the deterioration of non-vital organs come the deterioration of the vital organs – because they are no longer supported optimum. This is where memory loss comes, heart problems, respiratory problems and so on.

Myth 3: If You Are Not Born With Creativity, You Can Never Have It

Innovation is in high demand in every field. The higher you go in the hierarchy of an organization, the more important creativity and innovation becomes. Unfortunately, because people think this is a born-trait, they do not pay attention to the means that could cultivate and enhance it.

Once again, as with all deep-rooted myths, this one too is based on a grain of truth. Yes, some people are born with it. But this is just as significant as you would say that some people are born with the gift of the gab. It does not mean the creativity cannot be enhanced at any time. The formal education system is designed in such a manner, that the mind does not pay too much attention on the creative aspect. Soon, the logical part of the brain completely takes over and the creative part goes dormant.

The keyword here is 'dormant' – which means it is NOT dead. Hence, it can be revived and built upon. Hence, if you are not among those whose creative juice flow at will, do not worry. You can – with a few exercises and effort – fire it into full capacity at any age.

There are many specifically designed exercises that will help you develop your creativity thinking skills. You could download a number of such exercises from the Net and keep practicing day after day. With every day that passes you will find that your creative side is growing. Here are a few easy, fast yet extremely powerful tips:

- Listen to symphony music.
- Dance freely to the music of your choice.
- Brainstorm often on any topic you prefer.
- Carry a small notepad with you all the time and jot down whatever at-that-time-brilliant idea you get. Less than 5-10% of these ideas are great in the real sense. But this is what can change the world.

- Learn ONE new word every day. Open the dictionary, pick up a word and thoroughly learn how to use it. At the end of the year you will have 365 new words in your vocabulary and your mind would be open to explore more.

- When faced with any problem, write it down and put it somewhere where you can see it 24x7. Your brain would find a solution for you; it will suddenly hit you from the blue.

- TV kills creativity; see it only for entertainment and fight addiction to watch it.

- Stay away from drugs. You might get a few creative streaks while on drugs; but the cost is way too high to pay.

- Read voraciously. Books force your brain to imagine as the words you are reading create realistic paintings of an imaginary world.

- Keep your brain active. Keep challenging it with trying to learn something new all the time. The more active your brain in, the more creative it will be.

- Doodle all the time. Have a pen and paper ready in front of you and keep doodling when you are on the phone or just listening to someone talking.

- Add something new to your routine or change it every once in a while. This will keep your brain active and promote creativity.

Myth 4: Longer Hours Means More Work Done

One of the most destructive myths of all, this is the reason why most people – especially those who work in the highly competitive field – are so excessively stressed. The truth is that putting in longer hours means you are using your time ineffectively.

If you find that you are constantly working after hours, it is time to take a long look at your routine and make some drastic changes. You will need to identify those activities that drain your time and kill your efficiency. Eight hours per day is way more than enough to complete your tasks – provided you are using your time effectively and efficiently.

To get you started, here is a list of top 10 times wasters. How many of these are on your daily routine? Pay attention to your schedule for a week, and you will clearly see all the time-wasters in your work. Eliminate these drainers, and you will find that an 8-hour day offers you plenty of time to complete your work without being stressed.

Little Or No Planning. You move through the day with no planning or time organization, you will end up running helter-skelter wasting more time than you spend on actual tasks at hand. Start your day with a simple, but comprehensive 'To Do' list, which you would have completed the night before. People who start the day writing a 'To do' list would agree that very often, this is one of the major time drain; you will find that half of the day is gone planning on what to put on that list. Best is to write down this list, just before you get turned on.

Procrastination of difficult/ least liked tasks. There is a repulsive feeling generated when you think about difficult or unpleasant tasks and to avoid the feeling, you would normally put off the task for as long as you can. However, the feeling does not go anywhere, for at the back of your mind you know that sooner or later you would have to do it. Hence, this thought and condition of mind would affect all the tasks you undertake until you complete this one task. The result is that you would lose your positive energy and in the process waste so much time going through the day with half-hearted effort.

Instead, attack the **task** you hate the most first thing in the morning and do not stop to do anything else until it is over. The completion of this task and the relief that it would give you knowing that the worst is over would enhance the positive energy within and help you get through the day at a high pace and optimal efficiency.

Interruptions by emails/ phone/ visits/ meetings/etc.. Interruption of the phone and email constitute approx 80% of the deflected time when you are applying to completing a task. Every time you answer your phone or reply to an email, your mind disconnects from the task at hand and applies it to the interruption. In other words, you can do a given task 80% faster if you cut off all the possible interruptions.

There is a simple solution to this. Get organized and let the relevant people know about it. Announce to everyone the time you are available for discussions/ meetings. Put your telephone on answering machine so you would need to pick only those calls that really cannot wait. Have all your emails give automated response that you will check your email at XX time during working days, so people would know when to expect an answer. Discourage colleagues from strolling in your room for a chat or coffee break.

Inability to delegate. You do not need to do everything yourself. You have to learn to delegate all those tasks that others can do as well if not better and relinquish control over the task. Delegation is the best way to cut the time and increase the efficiency of completing any given task as this will ensure that you remain focused on the matters that require your specific talents and attention. It is easy to see how this would cut off the time of completion of your work and increase the overall efficiency.

Meetings that are NOT necessary (often an email would do just as fine) – try to discourage a culture where everything requires a meeting to move forward. Meetings unless these are for overall direction and goal setting – which normally should be no often than once in 3 months, preferably once 6 months – are a horrid drain of time. Try using group emails or memos instead. Choose a way that would bring you the results in the fastest possible manner.

Multitasking. You need to focus on what you are doing 100%. Only then you would be able to complete the task well and fast. Multitasking dilutes your focus and put is a start-restart mode where your brain would have to reload and reach to X-state every time you change your focus.

This start-restart mode tires the brain and lack of focus prevents you from doing your best at whatever task you are taking up.

Therefore, **multi-tasking** – while it is an excellent skill – drains away time and often even the effectiveness of delivering any task. Do not multi-task; do not encourage others on your team to multi-task unless it is strictly necessary. Build awareness around you why multi-tasking is not desirable

Inability to say 'no'. You have to learn to say 'no' when you want to say 'no'. Do not take up an X project because the boss requested you to do it; do not take up your colleagues work, because he requested you to fill in; do not do anything you do not want to do. Learn to say 'no' politely and firmly.

This is an acquired skill, so you will need to constantly practice on the tone, choice of words, reason to decline and various ways of stressing that you are serious. Learning you say 'no' will free a huge chunk of your time. But once you do it, you would not only be able to cover more but also much more efficient. You would also improve on your relationships as saying 'no' would set things right and leave no space for ambiguity or strained feelings.

Lack of exercise. You hear people saying all the time that they cannot exercise because they have no time; it is the other way round. You do not have time, because you are not exercising. Exercising triggers feel-good hormones in the brain and activates the body with positive energy. Put in a 30 minute brisk walk in the morning preferably – but it can be anytime you want — and see the difference this brings to your mind and efficiency.

You have no time to do 'nothing' — this is not a typographical error. It was meant to read 'nothing'. Unless you have time to do nothing, you are NOT spending your time right. If you are organized well, and get to spend your time right you will have every day some time to do nothing. At the worst, you could have the 'nothing' to do over the weekend; but it is best if you do it every day. When you are busy throughout the day and you do not get any off time, your brain will be too busy to relax even at night. If you do not relax, you would not be able to work with your full efficiency the next day; and the vicious circle sets in.

You have clutter all over — one major time drain — and mental drain as well — is clutter. Look around you — both at your work and at home — and if you find clutter, it is time you remove it all. Get rid of all the clutter around you and you will find things whenever you want immediately. Did you know that people spend $1/3^{rd}$ of their working time searching for something? Imagine the time you could save by having things organized and neatly placed where they are supposed to be.

Myth 5: You Need To Put In More Hours If You Want To Get That Promotion

There is a wrong assumption that you need to put in more hours of work to get noticed by your boss, so you would be nominated for that promotion. This is of course, one of the most popular myths that especially young people believe. The truth is different. It does not really matter how many hours you are putting in as much as what the outcome of your work is. In fact, if your boss is worth his salt, he will take the long hours as a sign of inefficiency rather than efficiency.

You want to get that promotion it is time you worked smart. Ensure that you have clear-cut goals and that you achieve them. A few tips to get the attention of your boss and get nominated for your promotion:

- Work in a team and be a good worker.
- Give credit for the contribution of others to the boss.
- Volunteer for the jobs that no one would take up – but which are important for the organization and your boss.
- Always ensure that your boss is shows in the right light to his bosses and in general among the team and his peers.
- Never badmouth the boss. Things like these have a knack of coming around.

- Be dependable. In other words, if a job is given to you, your boss should be able to forget about it because he'd confident that you would have it happen.

- Be friendly and help anyone who needs help around you. Of course, not at the cost the quality of your work; but be friendly and approachable.

- Work hard, stay focused on your job and always under promise and over deliver.

- Show your boss you are interested to grow, to do more, to take on more responsibility.

Myth 6: Delegation Means You Are Losing Control On Your Task

It is a myth that people who delegate work cannot do the work themselves. The truth is that they are smart enough not to waste their valuable time on tasks that others could do better. In this way, they could focus on the part of the task that would benefit most of their attention, experience and expertise. Delegation of work does not come easy so do not be hard on yourself when at first you find it difficult to let go of the total control you had on the job.

To get into the habit, delegate small and unimportant tasks at first and gradually let go of control until you have retained with you only that task that no one but you would do best. Once you learned to delegate you would find that you can achieve more in less time and that the work you complete is of the highest of quality.

Myth 7: If You Relax At Work You Are Seen As Frivolous

Many people tend to overdo it at work thinking that if they relax anytime and are seen relaxing, they would be taken as frivolous. It does not need to be that way. Of course, if every time someone is looking for you, you are found in the coffee lounge or gossiping with colleagues that would indeed become the impression. However, if you are paying attention to your work and are diligent with your responsibilities – it would actually be a good idea to take a few breaks from work during your workday.

Use these breaks to have coffee, talk to your colleagues, play a game on your computer – whatever relaxes you. Do not worry about anyone thinking you are wasting your time; people who work hard are spotted from afar. If you are serious about your work, your reputation will precede you.

Myth 8: Taking Work Home Will Help You Stay Ahead

Nothing is accomplished by taking your work home other than missing out on quality time with your family. Yes, you would be able to complete that project – but at what cost? It is necessary for the brain to recharge itself and thus it does when it is unwinding post work hours. When you carry your work at home, that is not the only thing you are carrying. You are also bringing all the tension and stress of the day back to your home. The result is that you would never get enough time to unwind and de-stress your mind. You would work late and go to bed thinking about work again.

In the morning next day, instead of waking up fresh and happy you would feel groggy and exhausted. Keep this up and you will be fatigued all the time throughout the day. Your efficiency would actually come down and your health you would be affected as well – especially your heart.

So, leave your work at your workplace; keep your home and office permanently separate. If there is additional work – and there would be times when this would happen – stay back in the office and finish it. When you leave your office your mind should be free of office work.

Myth 9: The Job Always Comes First

Yes, the job is a very important part of your life and it should have high priority in your life; but it definitely is not the No.1 thing. The No.1 thing is YOU; then comes, No.2 YOUR FAMILY and on the far No.3 is YOUR JOB. The person who puts the job first is in for some great disappointment for the job does not take care of you. You take care of the job.

When you put yourself on No.1, you would ensure that you are constantly improving yourself and preparing to move forward. You ensure that you stay healthy, happy and well fit with the job you are delivering. You come always first; your health, your happiness, your comfort. From time to time, when it is required, you might compromise a little on these aspects of your job – but this would be an 'it happens sometimes'.

Then, you have your family. You need to pay attention to your family, their needs, their feelings and especially their time with you. The job, should be the third on the list for this is the means that will keep your family and yourself happy and secure.

Unless you have your priorities right, you would not be able to advance in your life, for the frustration of working too much and sacrificing your family to the altar of your job, would get to you sooner than later.

Myth 10: To Get Ahead You Have To Please Your Boss

It is true that it is important that your boss like you and appreciates what you are doing. However, you definitely need not be a 'Yes man' to get ahead in life. Most bosses appreciate someone who can speak their mind; provided the opinion is given in moderation (not in a condescending way). Working hard is a better method to get ahead than polishing the apple.

This means you need not say 'yes' to your boss for anything you do not want to do. Juts learn to decline stuff politely. It is actually very important that you learn to "manage" your boss. In other words, learn to earn the respect of your boss – not be a slave who does whatever he says. The person who earns the boss' respect would be the one he would recommend for the promotion; the slave usually is passed up when the promotion comes up because the boss is too comfortable being pampered by this slave.

10 Tips to improve your productivity at Work

The main reason why most people put in long hours at work is because they are worried that they are not doing enough. Do keep in mind that 8 hours are enough to do a great job – and that you need not take your work home to advance your career or to ensure that work is done. If you are doing that, you are not productive enough in your work place. Here are some great tips that will improve your productivity.

1. Have Scheduled Breaks

It was mentioned earlier that taking breaks actually increases productivity at work. Your brain can do so much – even if you are super intelligent. That's why, it needs to recharge from time to time and this recharging is done through breaks. By "breaks" it does mean that you should get up from your seat and move about for a few minutes– though this is a good thing to do.

Mind-Relaxation Break

It could be just playing a game on your computer or mobile phone (ensure that there are no rules against this in your company). You could read a few pages of your favorite book, solve a crossword, have a cup of coffee/ fruit juice/ or just sip a glass of water, read a few jokes – do whatever relaxes you a bit and takes your mind off work.

The 20 Minute Catnap - Your Secret Energizer

If it is possible you could take a catnap of 20 minutes at lunch time. Twenty minutes is the exact duration which will actually charge you up for the rest of the day. Initially, you could set an alarm; after a while, your mind would be programmed to sleep exactly 20 minutes.

You will find that besides recharging your vigor, the catnap provides a host of health benefits such as lowering your stress levels, cholesterol and blood pressure and improves alertness and brain function. The best time to nap for early risers (larks) is between 1.00 pm and 2.00 pm; for late risers (owls) is between 2.00 pm and 3.00 pm.

To ensure that you get the maximum benefit from this exercise, drink coffee just before you take the nap. The cup of coffee would take about 20 minutes to kick in – just in time for the time when you are waking up.

Yearly Family Vacation

Do plan early for your yearly vacation. You may not go anywhere; you may like to use the off time to just stay at home with your family. Vacation time is a must-have at least once a year. To ensure that you do get your time off, talk it out with your boss and get his agreement for a mutually convenient time. Some bosses like it to grant leave when they are not around; others like the employees to be around to keep the office work running smooth when he is not there. Talking it out with your boss in advance would give you all the time in the world to ensure that by the time the vacation time comes up, all the important and urgent work is taken care of.

Flexi-timing Daily Offs

Work it out with your boss to offer you time off when you need it, allowing you to make up for it with long hours the next day. For example, if you want to have a relaxed lunch with your friend offer to put in 1-2 hours more that day evening or the next day. In this way, you need not take leave for the whole day when you actually need 1-2 hours off. This will ensure that you do not feel guilty about asking off-time and allows you to take care of yours more effectively.

When your personal needs are resolved, you will find that you are more relaxed, happier and definitely more productive.

2. Communicate, Communicate, Communicate

Communication is a great tool at work place and other places as well. At work however, it is extremely important that you communicate with everyone clearly and as often as it is required. To increase your productivity you need to communicate clearly with your boss, teammates and everyone else at work place.

When you share your tasks with your team members ensure that everyone understands exactly what each one is supposed to do.

Communicate with your boss about the progress of each given task. Some bosses like to know everything; they are micro managers. In such a case, you keep him updated as much as possible on all aspects of the job at hand. Otherwise, go to him only when you need special guidance/ permission or inform him about anything that required a change of plans.

Communication at the workplace does not mean 'talk about jobs' all the time. Communication also means saying 'thank you', 'sorry', 'please help me' as and when required. In other words, you should build a great rapport with your colleagues so when the time comes they will cooperate with you to get a job done, as you would with them. Productivity is often a definition that involved more than one person. The better you connect with your colleagues, the better your work will turn out.

3. Get Technology Savvy

Technology can make your life very easy and definitely increase your productivity at work. Use all the technology you can in your day to day work. Invest in a great smart phone that can stay in synch with the office computer.

Use your phone/ computer for personal memos that remind you about important 'to do' tasks.

Learnt to use your computer to optimize the quality of your and make your day easier. Use all the software you need to keep you doing your work best, and use it well. Your phone and your computer are not just fancy gadgets; they are to be used to the maximum extent. If you are not computer savvy, take a course and get computer savvy. Learn all that is to learn about your Smartphone and use them to make your work easier, faster and better. That is what these gadgets are for, by the way.

4. Music In The Background Is Good

It was found that playing music softly in the background improves concentration and productivity significantly. For best results use classic symphonies of Mozart, Bach, Beethoven and so on. Studies have shown that people who work with music or white noise in the background are able to focus better and work more efficiently.

5. Keep Clutter Off

One of the greatest killers of productivity is a cluttered office. If you take 15-30 minutes to find a document or information you need, you can imagine what this could do to your schedule. Take time off every day – ½ hour before you leave your workplace – and file everything where it should be and put your office in order. The organization of your office should be such that you should know where things are with eyes closed.

The same goes for your computer. Many people save files on their desktop and forget about it. When they need information they struggle through a mountain of electronic documents. It is very time taking and counter-productive if you have to search through every file in your computer until you find the right document to attach or refer; even worse, you may use/ send the wrong file.

Clutter saps positive energy and drain you. Have you felt fatigued when you see papers and files everywhere? This is because clutter accumulates negative energy and drains away positive energy. When your mind is filled with clutter, you cannot be creative, you cannot focus, and you cannot keep up your concentration. In other words, your productivity falls drastically if and when you are surrounded by clutter – whether this is in the office or on your computer.

A de-cluttered computer and office would increase your productivity and help you do a better job.

6. Delegate And/ Or Outsource As Much As You Can

Delegating and/ or outsourcing your work is one of the best ways to ensure that you increase your production and the quality of your work. When you get a task, take a long look at it and divide into two major parts. The first is that part of the task that you can do to perfection; the second part is what you could delegate.

When you delegate part of the work, you are getting rid of the "clutter" of the task and keeping only what you could do perfectly. Delegation/ outsourcing would have you give the highest quality time to the core part of the job; the delegated parts will also be done to perfection for their would be delegated to the best hands that can do them. The result is that everything is done faster, better and the least effort.

For delegation, look at your peers or subalterns. There would enough people around you whom you could delegate some parts of the job; what remains, if that still requires to be passed on, outsource. Keep only that part that you can do to perfection. For outsourcing you could use any of the available platforms who could put you in touch with the best of freelancers at a very affordable price.

7. Prepare For Your Task And Prepare For It Well

Pre-task preparations are very important if you want to do a good job faster. Let us say you are working on a marketing campaign. Before you sit down to do it, you should get all the data you need, all the reports you need to refer, all the number, figures, charts, marketing research reports and so on. In other words, have everything at hand that you require, so once you sit down to put together that marketing strategy, you need not get up from your desk for nothing.

The preparation might take time – but once it is done, your task will be a walk in the park. If you have not prepared for it, every time you need something you need to stop and search for it. Every time you stop and start you lose the thread of your thought and you will waste time getting "into it" again. In this way, you would spend twice or thrice the time doing the same task. Hence, to ensure optimum efficiency and productivity pay attention to the preparatory phase of your task.

8. Try Getting More Hours Out Of Your Day

Sometimes, you really need a little more time in your day. If you find that you are always running short of time, and are overwhelmed about the tasks you have at hand for lack of time, try getting a few more hours to your day with these tips:

Wake up 1 hour earlier than you normally do and go to sleep 1 hour later. In this way, you will have 2 more hours extra to your day. However, ensure that you do not sleep-less time than you need, which would be 4-6 hours per night.

Cut your showering time to half;

Shop online and cut the time you would have otherwise needed to commute, be in queue for paying, and so on;

Get a high-speed Internet connection;

Get the best-you-can-buy smart phones that have Internet on them, GPS and other applications that make your life easier – and definitely faster;

Use Sunday to plan your meals for the week. Make 1-2 packets that can be tossed in the micro oven for a meal, and store in the fridge. In this way, you will save a lot of time during the week as you do not have to think 'what do I eat tonight'. Have sandwich ready cold cuts in the fridge for a healthy and fast to put together lunch every day. It will save you both money and time.

Invest in a good automatic coffee/ tea machine;

Try working from home two days a week. You will need to convince your boss about this – and this might take some time, but it would well worth the trouble.

9. Cut Down Your Time on the Phone

The phone is the highest drainer of your time. Stop talking on the phone for hours on end "catching up". Instead, suggest you get together over the weekend or any other suitable day and have fun. Skype, video chatting, and other such applications have made it very easy for people to talk on the phone for hours on end – since most of these applications allow free over-the-Internet talk time.

However, this could be draining your productive time. Hence, do not shy away saying that "this is not a good time and hence, let us catch up over the weekend" to all those who love super long phone conversations. Keep the phone as a gadget for crisp communications rather than building a social network. Use your email for that; and meet people in person as much as possible.

Install a caller id and answering machine both at home and at work. In this way, you would know who called you when and you could call back when you are relatively free. You would not need to allow interruptions to your work to answer the phone.

10. Ensure You Have A Good Sleep At Night

There is a very important connection between a good night's sleep and productivity. A good night's sleep will allow your brain cells to recharge themselves and hence, when you wake up the next day, you would be "as good as new". It is very important that you get enough sleep. An adult needs about 4-6 hours sleep every night. You could check out and see exactly how much time of sleep you need – and ensure that you have that much sleep every night.

To ensure high quality sleep that rests and rejuvenates your mind and body take the following steps:

Keep distractions away from your bedroom. Have a rule that saying 'no work will ever go into the bedroom'. And stick to that rule as if your life depended on it.

Ensure that your bedroom allows you for complete quiet at night. Noise can interfere heavily with the quality of your sleep. In case, you live in a place that is noisy, invest in sound insulating your bedroom. You can also have a device that plays music at night as white noise to cover for other noises. Having the TV on for the night for the white noise is not a good idea for the TV light – which flickers in intensity – would not allow you to sleep well.

Finish your dinner at least 4 hours before your bedtime. Digestion slows down when you sleep and if you eat too close to your bedtime, you would end with indigestion, which will in turn interfere with your sleep.

Make it a habit to sleep at the same time and wake at the same time even during the weekends. In this way to set your body clock and get more out of your sleep because REM (rapid eye movement) takes place about 20 minutes before your normal waking time; and if you keep changing that you will miss out on REM. As a result, no matter how long you sleep, you will still feel fatigued and wasted.

Do not exercise too close to your bedtime, nor should you drink coffee.

Have a hot shower before turning in, as this relaxes the muscles and will give you a restful sleep.

Put your phone on silent mode until your waking time.

Wear loose and comfortable pajamas while sleeping; avoid any tight clothing.

Ensure that the room is dark when you go to sleep. In case you are among those people who are not comfortable in the dark, have a low intensity night lamp on.

Waking Up Exercise For 30 Minutes

Immediately as you wake up, do not reach out for that coffee. Instead, do some warming up exercises and then go for about 30 minutes intense exercising. This could be running/ jogging/ walking on the treadmill, aerobics, or whatever exercises you are into. Yoga is a very good alternative as well. In case you do not have an exercise regime worked out, try the Burpee.

What Is A Burpee?

Ridiculously simple, the Burpee is a set of exercises that works your full body. Because it is so simple anyone can start doing right away; it requires no training or guidance for there is no learning curve involved here. This is one exercise that provides 3 key benefits to the body:

It Builds Strength – the Burpee will work every muscle in your body enhancing its strength, i.e. the ABS, hamstrings, things, front deltoids, arms and chest. This set of exercises is so powerful that it is quoted as a favorite of athletes, military and body builders as well.

It Burns Fat – this set of exercises will burn about 50 percent more fat than the regular exercises in lesser time. The Burpee will accelerate your metabolic rate and keep it in top gear so you will burn more calories throughout the day. This is the ideal exercise if you want to lose weight fast.

It conditions muscles – the Burpee is compared to intense workouts because it is able to exercise each muscle in the body that counts. Take the 100 day Burpee challenge and you will know its power firsthand. This is very simple: do 1 Burpee on Day1, 2 Burpees on Day 2 and so on until on Day 100 you would do 100. Your body would feel like it is made of steel at the end of it, plus you would have built a phenomenal shape and strength.

What Are The Exercises That Go Into A Burpee?

This exercise set involves four steps:

Start from a squat position; keep your hands in front of you touching the floor

With one smooth jump, get your feet to back in the position of a push-up

Jump back to the squat position with which you started

From this position jump up in the air as high as you can

To enjoy the benefits of this exercise set to the maximum, these steps have to be made in very quick succession. You can see how to perform a Burpee here - http://www.youtube.com/watch?v=ynIxXvpdiLl for a straight set and http://www.youtube.com/watch?v=k43pjRs1mL8 for Burpee with variations.

Eat Breakfast Every Day

Eating breakfast is a very important way to start the day. Now only it would help you keep your weight in check, it would also help you get through the day with the highest levels of energy and efficiency. Do not skip the breakfast because you woke up late. Grab a sandwich, have some cookies with milk or simply have the a smoothie. There are 1001 smoothie recipes on the Net; download a few and keep them handy for days when you want to have breakfast in a hurry.

Do not miss this meal for this meal really makes a lot difference in the way your day shapes up. Fruits are an excellent choice, but you could eat anything you like. The saying, "Eat breakfast like a king, lunch like a prince and dine like a pauper" is a good one to follow.

You need to get back in control

The first step you need to take when you find that stress is taking over is to gain control on it. Stress is what could your mind, misguides your feeling, forces you to react in a destructive manner against yourself and against all you hold dear. Stress destroys your peace of mind and robs you of your health. It is like the equation between smile and frowning. You cannot smile if you are frowning; and you cannot frown if you are smiling. Try it – you will agree with me.

How to tackle stress? It is difficult; because it takes over all aspects of your life and hence, to eliminate it you will need to completely revamp your lifestyle. This requires nerves of steel, unshakable will power and a lot of time. It has to be done; and you need to embark on this journey as soon as you can; the sooner the better. Before you plunge headlong onto this trip you need to arm yourself with one of the most powerful tools against stress – meditation.

This is one tool that will strengthen you to fight against stress, will teach you to identify what is important in life and what is not and give you the power to choose the right path (and stay on it) to regain your work-life balance. Today, meditation is the need of the day for it is the only foolproof stress buster tool that anyone can master and use at will.

Contrary to common belief, meditation is not difficult nor it is time consuming. It is a technique that will help you gain control of your thought process, perception, and reaction to every external stimulus. It will also give you the power of "seeing the larger picture" and hence, prevent you from hyperventilating on every "small issue" in your life. It helps you take a step back and look at everything removed from the feelings the situation stirs. Meditation is the ONLY TOOL that will always stand you good when you want to put your life in order.

Meditation As a Tool Against Stress

In spite of all the advantages that seem to be derived from meditation, relaxation and de-stressing of the mind (and body) still seems to be the leading reason why people start on the quest to master meditation. When we talk about stress, what do you understand by it? What is stress in your opinion; from your point of view? How does it affect YOU?

What Is Stress?

When attempting to define stress, let us take a close look at what the definition is according to the Oxford dictionary: it says there that stress is "a state of affairs involving demand on physical or mental energy". Medical terms describe it as "perturbation of the body's homeostasis" and in simple, layperson's language it can be explained as "a state in which the mind and/or the body has to cope with exigent demands both from external and internal environs".

Every one, no exception (except perhaps saints or holy people), come face to face with stress at one point or the other in their lives. Things such tight deadlines at the workplace, economic crunch versus consumerism, traffic jams, growing children, the responsibility of caring for the aged, difficult relationships, marriage issues, staying single issues and the list can go on and on – are all stress factors. Fortunately, we all have an inbuilt mechanism to cope with a certain amount of stress. This usually acts like a fuse box, which is conditioned to shut down in case of overload. However, if the system overloads too often, chances are that some damage trickles up into the main system.

What happens when you go through any type of stress? From above you understand that stress is something that agitates you in some way or other. When anything challenges the body, the brain goes into defensive action. It shuts down logic and goes into the primitive mode of fight or flight response. As a result, your hormones raise blood pressure and prepare you to fight it out or run. The extra hormones and chemicals released in your blood are meant for primitive reactions, which today are not always applicable or workable. As a result, what happens? The chemicals and excess hormones remain in the blood and keep the body in a continuous "alarm" state.

As a result, you seem distracted, confused, have tense muscles, experience headache, backache and often even chest pain, and rapid pulse among others. It is needless to say that if you kept your body in this mode, you invite illness both mental and physical. Some of the diseases triggered directly by stress are irritable bowel syndrome, insomnia, hypertension, back pain, arthritis, diabetes, heart problems, and respiratory problems such as asthma, allergies and many others.

Meditation's Impact On Stress

As stress is basically the result of a chain of chemical reactions in your body, meditation is the reversal of that chain of chemical reactions. The relaxation that is induced by meditation creates a "feel good" factor that reverses the negativity of stress and its impact on the body. Meditation, as many research studies show, can reverse many serious disorders specifically caused by stress such as high blood pressure, heart problems, autoimmune disorders, aging, loss of concentration and memory, migraines, chronic pain and inflammation, among others. Most of all meditation helps in managing anger and depression.

According to brain mapping, the left frontal area is associated with a cheerful demeanor and the ability of positive interaction with people, while the right frontal area is associated with anger, introvert behavior and stress. In fact, a couple of centuries ago the right frontal lobe was removed surgically in people who were considered a threat through violent behavior. This is because this area of the brain has been associated (even then) with aggression, stress, negative reaction to surrounding environs. This is the same side that is also responsible for proper digestion, regulation of blood pressure and other such functions that are involuntary. Meditation is able to modulate this part of the brain and reverse the reaction of the autonomic nervous system.

People who meditate show an undeniable shift from the right to the left side of the frontal brain, changing their personalities from dark, foreboding and aggressive, and bent on self-destruction human beings to cheerful, relaxed, productive persons. The relaxation of the mind triggers a huge chain reaction in the body, which improves the functionality and effectiveness of all the systems in the body and sharpens the mind.

It is definitely not easy to reach the ideal state of meditation, nor to be able to invoke its benefits at will. Dr Steven Handling (Irvine, California) who has been practicing clinical psychology for two and half decades opines, "It may be a struggle to overcome the internal chatter that we all experience", but as a leading psychologist Roger Thomson, PhD (Chicago), says, (meditation) "... is a very effective stress-reducer... If someone is struggling with feelings of anxiety, he or she may benefit from its calming aspects. It's becoming absolutely necessary since it facilitates mental health because it brings about a higher level of self-acceptance and insight about himself or herself."

Many experts advise a combination of meditation and psychotherapy as the best way to control stress and keep a lid on it. Dr Thompson, who is also practicing Zen meditation for quite a while, opines that meditation and psychoanalytical theories are not too different from one another. They both "encourage its practitioners to become aware of the fundamentally distorted aspects of an overly individualistic view of human experience. Recognizing that the true nature of all individuals is emphatically non-individual, neither lasting nor separate, is the wisdom of Zen." He added, "In both meditation and psychotherapy, we are trying not to get caught up in internal preoccupation, but to be intimately present with what is happening here and now."

The findings that meditation is indeed an exceptional tool to fight stress and its negative effects on the body are substantiated by many studies. Often, just 7-8 weeks after meditation commenced the signs of anxiety, confusion, anger and depression were reduced considerably. As you gain experience, you would also feel more energetic; have an excellent appetite and digestion and reverse heart problems.

Mediation – A Permanent Way To Eliminate Stress

Spirituality has always been there as an integral part of the human civilization and evolution. Somewhere along the line, as the humanity became too engrossed in technology, science and their application, they moved away from it and the result appears to be catastrophic. Statistics show that about 70-90 percent of people who visit their medical practitioners for some or other disorder, find that it was caused by stress. The United Nations Report (1992), names stress as "the 20th Century disease"; on the same lines, the World Health Organization forecasts that it would become a "worldwide epidemic". The cost of stress in the USA is estimated to be about US $300 billion every year caused by absenteeism, decreased productivity, high employee turnover, accidents, medical and legal costs and other related matters. Out of all these, at least 60 percent ends up in chronic depression, suicide and other self-destructive state of mind.

It looks like living in the present is the only way to stay alive, not only happy. Happiness too, is a state of mind. It is a way of perceiving and reacting at external stimuli. It is a method by which you decide how to react to anything that happens to you. It may seem often that decision is not yours to make, as your feelings steer you to reactive actions. But this is where meditation is meant to help you; it trains to control your mind, your feelings, your reactions, your state of mind.

The "enlightenment" that you find mentioned so often in relation to meditation is nothing but the complete internalization that nothing really matters and therefore nothing should disturb you since you are part of a huge greater whole, which is constant. This is the state of no ego; the state where you realize that you as an individual do not exist unless you see yourself as a part of the whole; and when you see yourself as a part of the whole, you realize that nothing that happens to you changes that and therefore encouraging any feeling other than bliss and ecstasy of finding this truth, no other feeling is worth the effort.

Meditation And Success And Prosperity

What, in your opinion, can influence and chart success for you? Let us say you want to be the best in your field, you want to have enough money, a lovely family, a good house, cars and in general all the comforts that come with today's consumerist lifestyle. Let us assume that you get everything you wished for. Do you think you would be happy? Do you think you would consider yourself successful? If you answer with an emphatic 'yes', explain to me why there are so many multi-billionaires, who suffer from depression; why they are perpetually seeking for love, comfort, emotional security? Why they would always agree that money is not everything and definitely not the only thing that matters in the end. If money does not matter in the end, what does?

Success, real success, is when you learn to live in the moment. This stage, which is also referred to as 'mindfulness', is a state where your mind is intentionally focused only on the present. When you achieve this state of mind, you are hit by the realization that you are a separate entity from your thoughts, and that you can "look" at your thoughts without letting them interfere with you. You literally awaken to this new experience where you are able to look at yourself with a completely non-judgmental awareness of the present. This state of mind is so powerful, that it is known to reduce the progress of HIV. If this is a result when you spend only a few minutes in the 'NOW', imagine what happens when you permanently live in a state of mindfulness.

You are wondering how mindfulness affects professional (and personal) success. Mindful people are able to shed off their insecurities, so they are happy, more content, happier, more exuberant. It is like, literally, someone turned on the lights. This is why mindful people are able to grow faster in whichever profession they are. They are able to turn criticism, negative of threatening behavior, into positive reactions. They are more tolerant, more open and more accessible for which their relationships too are rewarding and satisfying.

It surely looks like the key to success and happiness and prosperity – in fact to all that is good – lies in the ability to live in the present. Well, how do you do this? The most beautiful description of the method to find the right way is a paradox. You need to let go of what you want so you could get it. If you want to take 'mindfulness' for its benefits, it kind of cancels itself because you are thinking of the future. You need to give up the thought of tomorrow completely and definitely and only see today, NOW.

Meditation And Grief

Grief is one of the most traumatic feelings of all. Losing someone or something precious is like losing part of ourselves. When your parents, spouse, children or a friend dies you would often feel the grief as physical pain. It hurts and it hurts badly. Meditation is said to be able to help you cope with your feelings. Can it help with grief? How?

Before I help you find answers to these questions, let me ask you to imagine the following scenario. Let us say that you live in the USA and you are happy and lucky to have your parents live nearby. You and your spouse are very fond of them as a result of which you visit each other often. Suddenly, one day, they announce that they would like to leave the USA and settle in Spain, where they feel they would enjoy their old age better. You would be deliriously happy for them, but for the fact that you would miss them terribly because of one peculiar condition – you can never see of communicating with them again once they are off to Spain.

How would feel after their departure? Sad, yes. Would you say you would be in grief? Definitely not. Why? Because, even though you would never speak with them or see them again, you know for sure that they were happy where they settled. Now, imagine that one day – instead of telling you that they are going to Spain, you are told that they both died in a car accident. Compare your reactions. Why do you experience heart-wrenching grief in the second case, while only sadness in the first case? The explanation is simple. The difference is because you know that your parents are happy wherever they are; they exist, even though you would not be able to reach them. In the second case, they would be lost to you forever.

Meditation brings to you the power of achieving mindfulness and with it comes the understanding and internalization of the truth that we all are one, part of one universe, one God. We come from it and go to it; manifestations of life might be different, but life is inextinguishable. Nothing is destroyed in Nature or Universe; it is only transformed. There is existence after death; life does not cease but changes in its form. Souls do not perish, the body does. Meditation has the power of making you believe this from within. You would still grieve, of course. But you would come to terms with it much faster than without meditation and your remedial actions would be positive, compassionate and deliberate (not reactive).

Meditation helps you accept your feelings, come to terms with them and move on by orienting your attention to the NOW. In other words, it helps you renew yourself from within.

Is Meditation The Best Tool For Stress

I hope this chapter has been an eye-opener for you. I also hope that when you are reading these lines, you would be convinced that meditation is the need-of-the-day for anyone who lives in the 21st Century. Meditation is not only for that person who is seeking spiritual enlightenment or the ability to trigger instant mind and body relaxation without drugs. Meditation is a way of living. You have to understand and fully internalize the principle of meditation before you start practicing it. You have to believe that it offers you entry into the realms within that you only thought possible with holy people.

If you look at what science says, meditation can be a tremendous boon for people that loose functions of certain parts of their body. The brain has the ability of rewiring itself provided it is exercised well enough. Research on meditation is still young and very controversial. However, there is something that everybody agrees to – meditation makes a person calmer and more tolerant of self and of others. By doing so, it helps de-stressing the body; stress being the topmost cause of inflammation, pain and auto-immune disease in the bodies of human beings today.

That it is useful in correcting health problems was known, even though it was not quite substantiated earlier through adequate scientifically approved studies. However, the discovery of the plasticity of the human brain points to other possibilities that could change humanity forever. You can train your brain to become compassionate, kind, tolerant, patient, happy and content.

In a world full of hatred, stress, aggression, suppression, terrorism, intimidation, the stronger-wins-the-weaker-perishes yard stick, consumerism, ambition, violence, lust, atheism among others – can there be anything better than meditation? In fact, like martial arts for self-defense, sex education and basic schooling, meditation too should be made compulsory in schools. This is a discipline that if adopted early enough can shape the minds of children and through them the world into a better place to live.

Meditation would teach humility and humbleness to humankind in an hour when it seems they reached the culmination of the haughtiness on their ability to play God through science. Meditation would keep that window open so you could compare yourself with the whole Universe and see that (i) you are an integral part of it, hence you are the Universe, and (ii) when your ego chooses to flare up, and you separate yourself from the Universe and become insignificantly small and powerless.

Meditation is indeed the answer today. Human beings need to learn to eliminate their ego and respect life in all forms. They also need to learn and internalize the fact that life (on Earth) is a transient energy, which continues beyond death. The truth about the continuum of existence, from this realm to another can teach you to lead a fuller life personally, professionally and spiritually.

Meditation is the path that can help you find God within and with this realization the importance of finding and living in the NOW would be amplified. Meditation would also help you achieve the status of contentment, one which the today's world almost completely wiped out.

Looking at all the above spillovers from meditation, I would whole-heartedly agree that "yes, meditation is the need of the hour, today; all over the world. Yes, this is the missing ingredient that could save this planet and human beings from a sure self-destruction path.

Six Baby Steps To Optimize Your Efficiency

1. You Want The Best Performance, Stop Thinking About It

You would have heard the saying, "Dance like no one is watching you…". Have you thought why? Have you tried it out? Try it. When you dance alone, you dance with complete abandon by letting the music dictate your movements without thinking whether you look awful, like a clown or clumsy. You dance for the joy of it, right? In majority of cases, such experience is amazing and leaves exceptional influence on your life. Do not think for one moment that mindfulness is leaving the world and getting into your head. No, on the contrary, it is seeing everything around you with heightened clarity and becoming part of it (completely blending in) without any judgment. Mindfulness removes the threat from negative feedback, so you can rise above it. The greatest obstacle in the path of success is evaluation of self and others and the fear of its outcome. As Dr Stephen Schuller (Psychologist, University of Pennsylvania) says, "Instead of getting stuck in your head worrying, you can let yourself go." It is then that you start seeing the actual thing you are doing and you can really focus on it – like it is the last thing on earth you would be doing. At such time, you forget about what others are talking about you, what they would say, or any evaluating or judgmental lens you would come under; all you would know and think about would be the task you have at hand. Needless to say, with such a focus and concentration, nothing but the best would be the outcome.

2. Tomorrow Might Never Be – Stop Worrying About It

The Holy Book points at the carefree life birds and animals are leading because they are not worried about tomorrow. They take every moment as it comes. I have not mentioned the Great Book to allude to religion here; rather I want to point out at the wisdom hidden in its pages. I was talking with a friend about my daughters' future and how worried I was because I had no savings put aside for them. He told me something I will remember for a very long time. He said, 'Hey, why worry? If they are capable and worthy of your love and affection they will grow into responsible young people, have good jobs and earn their comforts – and therefore your money would have no meaning for them; if they are hopeless and unworthy of your love they would grow into irresponsible young people who would not value money or your love – therefore, once again they your money would have no meaning for them.' Just look at one day in your life. What occupied your attention the greatest part of the day? You would be surprised to answer – the future. This future may not be distant; but it would be the future nonetheless. "What would my boss say about this job?", "What will I do for dinner tonight?" and things like that. We hardly live in the present moment. The unrest you feel is stress mounting from the anxiety brought on by your incessant thinking of the future. Just stop and concentrate on NOW – all these thoughts would disappear and what you would be left with would be an unimaginable tranquil space; an amazing experience that would never end, because you would always be in the NOW.

3. When Overwhelmed About The Future, Focus On Your Breathing

You would have heard your grandmother or mother advice you to count until 10 if you are angry with someone, before you say or do anything about it. Others would tell you to take a few long and deep breaths when you feel angry or aggressive; it is said that this has a calming effect. Indeed it does. How? It brings you into the NOW and when you are in the NOW your ego is no longer the most important thing for you. You do not feel threatened or intimidated by the behavior of others. This time gap where you redirect your concentration, give you a window to escape from reactive action to a thoughtful one. Look at these sayings: "Anger is just one letter short of danger", "Anger is temporary insanity", "Anger makes you blind to reason." They all say one thing – when in anger you loose control. Mindfulness, that you get through breathing, would give you time to regain self-control and separate yourself from your ego. The result is amazing, even when you are prepared for it. You feel detached, in full control and surprisingly no anger.

4. To Master Time, You Need To Lose Yourself Into It

There is a beautiful story in the Indian Epic, "The Mahabharata" where Arjun who was described as the best archer in the whole world. When all the pupils complained to their Guru (teacher) that bestowing such an honor on Arjun might not be without prejudice, the Guru lined all of them up for a test to prove his point. He hung a fish on a tree very high up and asked the pupils to hit its eye. He also instructed that before they should take aim and wait for his orders before shooting.

All the pupils lined up and the Guru went from one to another asking them what they were looking (they were ready to shoot arrows at the time of the question). The first one said, he saw the tree, the sky above, the branches of the tree, the birds flying around, the fish, the thread by which it was tied up and its eye. The Guru told him to leave. The second pupil said, he saw the tree, the branch, the fish and its eye. The Guru told him to leave as well. He reached Arjun and asked him what he saw. Arjun replied, "Guru ji (respectful way of addressing a teacher), I can see nothing but the eye." The Guru smiled and told the pupils, a great archer see nothing other than his target, nothing at all. This is the reason Arjun is considered one of the greatest archers in the world.

In our connotation, you need to immerse yourself in the present. When you do so, you would be so enveloped by that NOW, that you would lose sense of time. This would happen to you, for example, when you do something you enjoy completely and you are so engrossed in it that when you look at the clock you blinked incredulously at the time elapsed. Living in the present would fill you so completely that you would be lost in the sensation.

5. Embrace The Problem, Not Run Away From It

When you are taught driving on dangerous roads, stunts, or racing one of the first things they will teach you is how to control a car, which skids out of control. While your reaction would be to jam breaks and freeze your hands on the steering wheel, the recommended action would be to roll with it. By allowing the car to roll with the skid, would give you back the control. Similarly, when you are hit by sadness, losses, and pain in life, never try to shun these feelings away. By doing so, you are focusing on the distress they cause you. Rather you roll with; accept the feelings as natural and then choose your next plan of action with the full understanding of the present.

Do not confuse acceptance of the present negative feelings with resignation to your fate. Accepting means you focus on what you are feeling without judgment accept the feelings and then take appropriate action to feel better. Resignation would be to accept the feelings and be stuck in their negativity.

6. Nothing Is Permanent So Why Hang On To Anything

If you see people who have married for 20 years or more you would be likely to see two people taking each other for granted. They feel they know what they other wants, does, says – everything. And one day, one of them dies. The remaining spouse would be caught up with the things he or she would have wanted to say or do – tomorrow, which now would never come.

Another example would be – you go to your workplace every day. Same route, same colleagues, more or less same work; days seems to merge into one another so much that you lose the ability to enjoy what you see or do. Stop one day and look again. Everything would be new now that you are taking time to notice. Familiar, yes; yet everything was new. You would not be able to say that "I am sure that this would be this way." You realize that anything can happen anytime, anywhere. Nothing is permanent; nothing is for sure - other than NOW.

There is another lovely example. This is a movie, the name of which escapes me, right now. Nicholas Cage plays the role of a psychic who could see just two ahead into the future. In a candid moment he turns to his girlfriend and say something like this, "Yes, I can look into the future, but I do not really know it. Because every time I look at it, it changes." This is actually summing the whole thing about NOW. You cannot be sure of anything at all, other than the present moment; yours NOW.

I am sure you are convinced by now of the importance of living in the NOW, at least for sometime, if not consistent. However, before you take up this endeavor let me tell you a secret. Living in NOW cannot be used as a goal; because when you do so you are thinking about the future and thereby killing it. Therefore, if you want to achieve mindfulness, just pay attention to the present and breathe. Everything else will fall into place. You will find yourself growing in awareness about your existence now; about how you feel vis-à-vis your environment, and everything that surrounds you; but you will loose track of time. You have arrived in your present. Welcome!

20 Work – Life Balance Ideas

We have learned a lot about various aspects of the work, relaxation, productivity and efficiency. It is time to look at some concrete ideas that will bring about work-life balance.

1. Leave Work Place On Time

Make up your mind and decide that from now onwards you will leave the office right on the dot – when your day is meant to end. To ensure that you can keep this promise, you need to plan your day in such a manner that you will have all the tasks on your 'to do' list done by that time.

Tip: Prioritize your work carefully. Have the important tasks completed early. Delegate as much as it is possible. At the end of the day, if you still have some tasks remaining, these would be of the lowest importance, and often they could be pushed to the next day or further delegated. Learn to recognize and separate which tasks HAVE to be completed and which tasks can be pushed to the next day.

2. Identify The Areas That Drain Your Time And Eliminate Them

Identify all the activities that drain your time and eliminate them one by one. Focus on getting as much as possible done during the day. Organize little rewards for yourself when you complete all the tasks that you have committed for the day. Keep in mind that taking a break is not the same as wasting time. A well deserved break would actually help you increase your efficiency and productivity.

3. Have A 'To Do' List On Your Table BEFORE You Leave Your Office

The workplace 'to do' list needs to be done in the office. Before your leaving time, consecrate 15 minutes to jot down your 'to do' list for tomorrow. It is very important that this step is followed strictly because your effectiveness for the next day depends on it. When you write down what you need to do, you will be preparing yourself mentally for tomorrow. This will make it easier to start the next day without wasting too much time in 'warming up' for the day.

4. As Much As Possible Use The Latest Technology To Increase Your Efficiency

There are plenty of applications that you could download and use for free that would help increase your productivity. Learn to use technology to your advantage. You can save a lot of time and effort with the right applications and online/ computer tools. You can synchronize your computer with your Smartphone so you could keep track of the tasks you have planned to complete.

It is worth investing time and effort to learn about as many as possible software programs (there are many free and easy to download) that could help you increase your productivity at work and on a personal front. It is important to keep in mind that if your personal matters are not in order, your work would suffer and vice-versa. Hence, you need to put things into the right perspective both on personal and work fronts.

There is a very long list of web tools, software programs and services that would help you increase your efficiency and productivity here – check it out - http://blog.workmonk.com/list-of-108-web-tools-services-and-softwares-to-increase-your-productivity-and-efficiency/.

Look for 'free tools to increase efficiency/ productivity' if you want more.

5. Let Everyone Know That You Are Not Available After Office Hours

Let your boss and colleagues know that you are not available to office work after outside office hours. For best segregation, you need to maintain two separate mobile phone numbers – one for the office personnel, clients and other work related contacts; and the other for your personal use. After you leave the office, switch your mobile phone to voicemail / answering machine informing the caller that you would definitely get back during office hours the next working day. This is a very important step that will help you segregate your personal and office life very effectively.

In order to have your boss and colleagues respect this aspect, you would need to build a solid reputation for yourself that you are a very effective and serious worker. If your boss is aware that you are putting all you can during the 8 hours you are at the workplace, he would not be likely to want to disturb you outside office hours.

6. Eat Light In The Office

A heavy meal would make you drowsy and lower your efficiency a great deal. Avoid heavy lunches at work. Rather have packed 6-8 medium sized sandwiches and keep nibbling throughout the day. This will keep your metabolism running and will ensure that you are alert and focused throughout the day.

Alternatively, you could pack a few light sandwiches for lunch and carry with you fruits and nuts to nibble upon the whole day long. This will keep your hunger pangs away, help you lose weight, and at the same time ensure that you are able to give your one hundred percent (and more) to your job.

7. Drink Less Coffee

Contrary to common belief coffee is NOT your best friend when it comes to maximizing your productivity. Actually, too much coffee has exactly the opposite effect. Excess coffee will keep you so high strung and excited that you would actually not be able to work too much. You would also experience other harmful symptoms such as irritation, inability to focus too long on one matter, easily excited and drawn into arguments, forgetfulness and so on.

You want to work at your maximum capacity – stay away from more than 2 cups of coffee per day. An easy way to see whether you are addicted to coffee is to ban for a whole day. If you find at any time that you crave for coffee, then you are addicted. Take measures to eliminate this addiction for good.

Instead of coffee – if you do want to drink something – drink green tea without sugar or with natural sweeteners (honey, aspartame, etc.). You can drink green

8. Stay Hydrated

Drinking water is very important for your body and – as not many would know – for our efficiency. When the body gets dehydrated the metabolism slows down and you feel lethargic. No matter how hard you try you would not be able to summon enough energy to get you through the day at the top of your productivity potential.

If you feel thirsty – you are already dehydrated. Look for other symptoms that you are suffering from lack of water in your system:

- dark colored urine - very limited in quantity;
- you feel sleepy, tired and irritated though you had a good sleep;
- you suffer from intermittent headaches;
- you are unable to understand the problem; you feel confused;
- your head is reeling
- your mouth is dry and feels like parchment.

How much water should keep you happily hydrated? About 2.5-3 liters would be good. Want to make it even better, add a little lemon to it. This will assure that you hydrate throughout the day.

9. Stay Realistic About Your Own Capacity

Do not take on more than you can chew. Be realistic about how much you could achieve every day. In case it is not possible for you to achieve something within the given deadline, say so in the beginning or at the first moment you realize that you need more time. As much as possible take on just as much work you can deliver with the best quality.

In case there are very demanding deadlines once in a while, it is worth suspending all your 'work-life balance principles' and get the work done. As an exception, it is okay; but NOT as a rule. If you see that the deadlines keep crossing the line into your personal time – and these are deadline that your organization has to deliver, ask for help or seek another job.

One of the worst thing to do, is to play 'Superman' and continue to push yourself beyond your limits to complete impossible deadlines. Such behavior would mean total burnout, which in turn would mean falling in efficiency, negative impact on your relationships and acute health distress. In other words, nothing good will come out of it – hence, IT IS NOT WORTH IT.

10. Actively Delegate Work

Delegating work and passing the buck are two different things. Do not feel guilty to pass on smaller tasks that make your main job to others in your office who could deliver the work better. Delegation of work will save you time and ensure that the overall task is done at maximum quality.

The trick to successful delegation of work is your way you do it. Here as a few must-do when you delegate work:

- Always be polite, realistic about the work you delegate.
- Always give credit for the work done.
- Always delegate only what the respective worker can do best (whatever the specialty of the worker).
- Do not hide the fact that you are delegating the work.

11. Take Short Breaks To Relax Mentally

You will achieve more if your mind is fresh and focused on the work. This does not happen if you are at it the whole of 8 hours you are at your work place. Take small breaks in between and as your mind relaxes a bit, you'll be able to give your 100% to the tasks you have on your hand. Taking 5-10 minutes long breaks every 2 hours will increase your productivity and efficiency manifold.

12. Always Help Others When Time Permits

Help your colleagues when they are stuck and you have the time. The key here is "when you have the time". If you have your own deadlines to meet – everyone is on its own. However, if you have the time, and someone in your office is hard pressed for time for meeting an important deadline, volunteer help – and ensure you do your best at the task you take on. Do this to anyone who genuinely stressed with work. The courtesy will be returned to you when you are in trouble – your colleagues would be happy to cooperate with you when you are in trouble with deadlines.

13. Keep Time Aside To Learn New Skills

It is very important that you improve at your job. There are 1001 things you could learn that could assist you professionally. Plan your time in such a manner that you get time to learn something new, something that would help you advance in your professional career.

Have personal career goals fixed to help you here. You need to have moved from point A to point B in 5 years. Unless you have clear goals for your professional growth and work systematically to achieve them, you will find yourself stagnating after a while, which will kill your efficiency and productivity.

To work best you need to constantly challenge yourself to do better, to move ahead, to conquer new horizons. One of the best ways to achieve work-life balance is to be happy with your work; and that happiness comes with the realization that you are doing well in your professional life.

14. Keep Personal And Professional Life Separate

No matter how tempting it is to mix the two, you need to keep work and personal life separate. Make strict non-negotiable rules that:

- You will NOT bring work home or take calls related to the office once you are at home;
- If you are on vacation, office is CLOSED and you are unreachable;
- At workplace, you do not encourage your spouse or children to call you unless it is an emergency;
- Do not take cut work short to pick up children from school or run errands for your spouse, unless you mean to compensate later with that amount of time;
- Do not entertain friends on work time (at lunch, coffee breaks, etc.).
- Let everyone at work know that you do not prefer to be contacted regarding official matter outside office hours;
- If your boss does not respect your homework life boundaries, look for another job.

15. Always Have A Positive Attitude

You will always achieve more if you have a positive attitude towards your life in general and your work in particular. Take every problem with a positive approach and look for solutions rather than excuses. Keep in mind this wonderful saying some wise person said, "People will be remembered for TWO things in life – for the problems they created and for the problems they solved."

- Be the problem solver in your work place.

- Always smile. It costs nothing and it improves at atmosphere around you drastically.

- Speak politely to everyone at your workplace, especially to those who do not deserve it. Courtesy is the sign of a mature and well-bred human being; lack of courtesy does not say much about the person.

- Always be ready to help – but keep track on your own deadlines and work;

- Always under-promise and over-deliver. This is the ladder to professional success. It applies both internally (to your boss/ colleagues) and externally (clients).

- Never gossip and encourage gossip (by listening, laughing, giving your two-bits about whatever is said). Gossip is the easiest way to poison relationship. Don't think that those who gossip about X, Y and Z would not gossip about you.

- Follow the rule of positive reinforcement for everyone. If you do not have something nice to say, don't say anything. You do NOT owe the truth to anyone. Develop the habit of giving a pat on the back whenever possible. Whenever you see something positive about your colleagues, junior and boss say it. Everyone loves appreciation. Keep in mind that there is a very thin line between flattery and appreciation. Do NOT flatter; appreciate.

16. Find A Job That You Love To Do

Initially, for the sake of your family or raising funds you might take on whatever job you find, wherever you find. Even so, ensure that you always give your best in whatever job you are. However, do not stop until you find the job you love; because it is only then that you would be able to give your 100% and be happy at the same time. When you find the job you love, your work will no longer be work – but pleasure and pleasure would never stress you.

17. Have A Comfortable Workplace

You are working 8 hours in a place; ensure that you are comfortable. Check on these matters – and this is NOT an all-inclusive list:

- Do you have proper lighting?

- Do you have a comfortable chair?
- Is your desk adequate for your requirement?
- Is there enough fresh air in your office?
- Is it comfortable temperature wise? In some offices where the air conditioning is centralized, it might be too cold or too hot. If so, look for ways to redress this matter.
- Do you have adequate tools to deliver your job? Is your laptop/ desktop working properly? Do you need anything else?
- Is there anything that needs improvement at your workplace – to ensure that you are 100% comfortable in your surroundings?
- Do you have colleagues around you who speak too loudly? Is there anything around you that disrupts your pace at work?

Unless you are mentally and physically comfortable at your work place you cannot give your 100%. Your efficiency and productivity are directly proportional to how comfortable you are. Ensure that you create a little island of comfort at your workplace. If you explain your problem to your boss vis-à-vis your ability to deliver/ productivity, you will get whatever you want – if that is possible within the budget. If not, look for another job for you are likely to feel frustrated sooner or later.

18. Invest In Latest Gadgets And Use Them Extensively

Technology today can reduce the workload by $2/3^{rd}$ if applied correctly. Today, it is the era of working smart; the working hard era is gone. Invest in the latest technology smart phone, laptop, latest software, or whatever tools you require to give your best in your job. Stay abreast with technology development – you will be able to work better, faster and use less time than you would otherwise.

You will find that the investment in these latest high-tech tools will more than pay for their cost.

19. Negotiate For Work At Home Days or Flexi-hours

If you can do your job from home, try negotiating with your boss for 2-3 days a week working from home. This will help you cut on the stress and time of commuting and give your best to your job. This is especially good if you need quiet and uninterrupted time for your task.

In case this is not possible, try negotiating Flexi-hours where you could come later and go later from your office. In this way, you could complete household chores and other important personal matters without the need of taking a day off from your job.

20. Saying 'No' Is Important

Learn to say 'no' and say 'no' whenever it is required without any qualms. More than 90% of your problems would not be there if you learn to say 'no' when you want to say 'no'. You are not in a popularity contest; you do NOT need to say 'yes' to everything that lands on your desk.

Conclusion

This book hopefully, will help you achieve the very challenging goal of perfect work-life balance. Agreed, many tips and advices given here are easier to say than done; but none are impossible. Make up your mind that you will work towards achieving this goal, break it up into smaller bite-sized goals and go for it. Look up the SMART goals principle; use this method to achieve work-life balance.

Do not be hard on yourself. It will be hard. This is an uphill task and you do not expect that that it will be easy. It will take time for you to manage your time as you want best. It will lots of effort; expect burnouts, frustration, and tough spots before you reach your goal. But stay on the path and it will happen. The rewards of finding that perfect work-life balance are huge; and worth every bit the effort you are putting in.

In case you are unable to find ways to perfect this work-life balance with your job, consider very seriously becoming an entrepreneur. Look for ways to set up a home business or become a freelancer/ consultant in the virtual world. In this way, you could work from home for any organization or employer in the world with the help of the high-speed Internet.

Remember – where there is a will, there is always a way. Look for it and you will find it. If you find a way, great; if not, make one. Either way, you get to achieve your goal.

When you do, you will find peace of mind for you will be able to enjoy the best of both worlds.